# a bouquet of poems

**Sara Arneberg**

a bouquet of poems

First Edition 2022

*a bouquet of poems*

Copyright © 2022 by Sara Arneberg
All rights reserved including the rights of reproduction
in whole or in any part or form.
Title of the original: *a bouquet of poems*

Illustrations: Sara Arneberg © 2022, All Rights
Reserved.
Cover: Sara Arneberg © 2022, All Rights Reserved.
Publisher: BoD - Books on Demand, Stockholm,
Sweden
Print: BoD - Books on Demand GmbH, Norderstedt,
Germany
ISBN: 978-91-8027-733-4

*To my closest friends*

# Poems in this collection

## Poems in this collection

# Will there always be rain?

Lips are broken, tears keep falling
with loss of friends, this girl is bawling

No words spoken, she's in such pain
after sunshine, will there always be rain?

Dawn is woken, when she wish she had
someone to hug, when things feel so, so bad

-s

# To all girls

Girl, stop crying
pick up your crown,
hold your head up high
and look at the sky

Dance like the clouds,
sing like the wind,
shine like the sun
and for once in your life,
have some good fun

-s

# A life

A heartbeat,
so loud but yet so silent

A voice,
so powerful but yet so powerless

A life,
so strong but yet so weak

We could change the world,
if we just dared to speak

-s

# Different but yet the same

You're the sun and I'm the moon,
like siblings in the universe
We float in space with so much grace
we make all others furious

Eyes are blue and eyes are brown,
like ice cold ice and caramel
We sing and dance at every chance
though it might sound kind of terrible

You're the sun and I'm the moon,
like siblings in the universe
We fight and scream but still we dream
and that's what makes us curious

-s

# A love poem

As much as the wind howls
and as much as the thunder rumbles,
I will always be there when life crumbles

As much as the sun shines
and as much as the rain pours,
I will always and forever be truly yours

-s

# There is this guy

There is this guy,
so nice and sweet
He stabs my heart,
I weep and weep

Still I do,
come back to him
When life is feeling,
really grim

Even though,
he hurts my soul
He also makes me,
feel so whole

There is this guy,
so brave, so bright
He starts to laugh,
and I take flight

-s

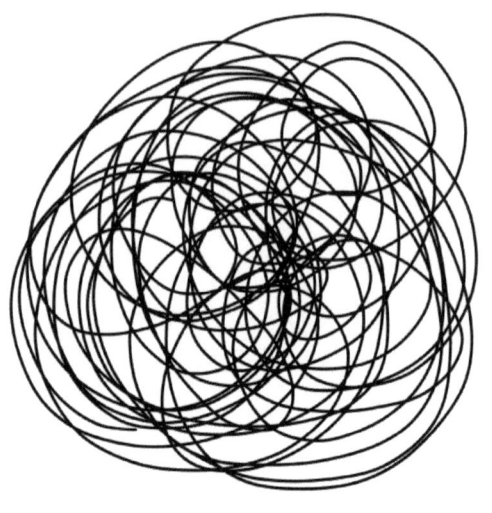

# The Color Gray

I feel so blank,
I feel so dead
though I know it's all just in my head

I feel so numb,
I feel such weight
You and I had a dreadful fate

I feel so empty,
I feel so pale
All because of your "needs" as male

I feel so lonely,
I feel so hollow
You say "do that" and I just follow

-s

# To live forever

To live forever,
and ever, and ever

To breathe wherever,
whenever, however

To be whoever,
whatever, whenever

That's what we all want,
though never and never

We aren't that clever,
that clever, that clever

To live forever,
and ever, and ever

-s

# Shower thoughts

Standing in shower,
for way too long
Music in head,
someone's favorite song

Water so hot,
my skin will turn red
The price that you'll pay
when you talk to the dead

Standing in shower,
for way to long
I wish you were here
but you're already gone

-s

# Astronaut love

I met someone sweet, someone bold, someone kind,
oh my dear lord how I wish he was mine

I saw him today, yesterday and last Friday,
with that light in his face from the big shiny moonray

I wish he could see me, and take all my love,
to hold and to care with the stars all above

To look in my eye and hug me so tight,
to say "why can't we, just stay here all night?"

I know that we're not, on the same page,
though the stars that unite us been here for some age

Oh my dear love, my greatest best friend,
please take this correctly, don't make my dream end

-s

# Scar

When you hold knife against arm,
you get strucked by this charm
A charm that will harm,
if you don't wake by alarm

The feeling of calm,
seems to come from a far
Though when you are done,
you'll be left with a scar

A scar to remind you,
of the nights you were weak
In the darkest of times,
when you happiness seek

-s

## Garlic bread

Garlic bread, I feel dead
crying here upon my bed

Toast with spice, eat a slice
maybe once, maybe twice

Garlic Bread, feel the dread
all the books I should have read

Tasty crust, is a must
when life's shit you can always trust

Garlic Bread, Garlic Bread
making all the tears unshred

-s

# I miss you

The closure I felt with you is nothing like I've
ever felt before
The way I locked my soul to your heart and my
mind to your eyes

The way you did the same but to me

The way we laughed, the way we cried,
the way we screamed
The way we hugged, the way we kissed,
the way we dreamed

And now you're gone, just like the wind
I'm all alone searching for another boy like you

To share, to hold, to be there for in need

But there is none, you're one of a kind
And that's probably why, I can't get you of my
mind

-s

# Apple pie

Today is a day, I just wanna die
The only thing keeping me,
is this piece of pie

Today is a day, I just wanna die
The stress is so high,
it could reach up the sky

Today is a day, I just wanna die
You said it would be better,
but boy did you lie

Today is a day, I just wanna die
If it weren't for this big piece of
fucking apple pie

-s

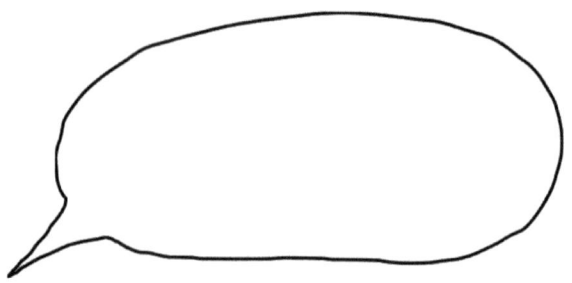

# Here with you

We hug a long time, you're holding me tight
I take a step back, your eyes look so bright

Then I watch you walk, away from my door
The weather so cold, you freeze to the core

I get filled with this feeling, of great emptiness
A feeling of lonely, that I can't suppress

I should have said that, I should have said this
Oh my dear friend, it's you that I'll miss

I don't know when, I will see you next
Though we'll probably talk a bit over text

Well, It's not the same and you know it too
Cause' the feeling of home is just here with you.

-s

## I wish I lived an 80's song

I wish I lived an 80's song,
walk around the city all day long

Singing, dancing, flirt a bit,
in the world's big greatest 80's hit

He and I take the same train,
then we're dancing in the rain

Soon I just wanna have some fun,
roller-skating in the sun

What a feeling that would be,
Dance with someone who loves me

I wish I lived an 80's song,
the one where everybody sings along

-s

## Never thought I would have fell for you

Never did I thought I would have fell for you,
your hair, your laugh, and everything that you do
But that snowy walk made something in me
click,
it was so ridiculous like a good old magic trick

Your eyes so deep with that sparkle of light,
your smile so big and enormously bright
The snow keeps falling, like I did for you,
What are you thinking? How I wish I knew

Never did I thought I would have fell for you,
your voice, your mind and all the other things too
How I'm longing for you to be by my side,
Everyday of our lives until one of us die

I want you to hold me and hug me so tight,
to keep me company for each and every night
I'm floating on clouds, 'cause you make me so
high
please grab my right hand and we'll fly to the
skies.

-s

# Do you love me all the same?

You, my dear, please forever stay
Stomach feel like butterflies, when I see you
every day

In hallway your eyes and mine, they meet
Feels like I'm walking on something else than
just concrete

When you stare, and I stare right back
I just know in that moment, it's gonna be this
great flashback

My only wonder is, do you love me all the same?
Are you the one who'll take care, of my small
but delicate flame?

Meet me in the daybreak and tell me what you
feel
Is it time for us, after all these years, to finally be
real?

And please do not forget, your smile and your
laughter
Then maybe, we can live forever happily ever
after

-s

## Woman

I was called a woman,
the first time I got my period
I was called a woman,
the first time at eleven
I was called a woman,
in the bathroom of the restaurant

I was called a woman,
when life was easy and school was fun
I was called a woman,
when gender didn't matter and norms did not
affect
I was called a woman,
with my hair still up in piggy tails

I was called a woman,
though all I really was were a child.

-s

# My name

I have never, really liked my name;
the length, the sound, it's all just lame

Though when you say it, it sounds just right;
like the wind, a late midsummer's night

The name of which that I respond,
is now a word, the earth beyond

A song, a piece, composed by you
each time you sang my trust just grew

One more time, please sing the tune;
and you see the butterflies will flutter soon

-s

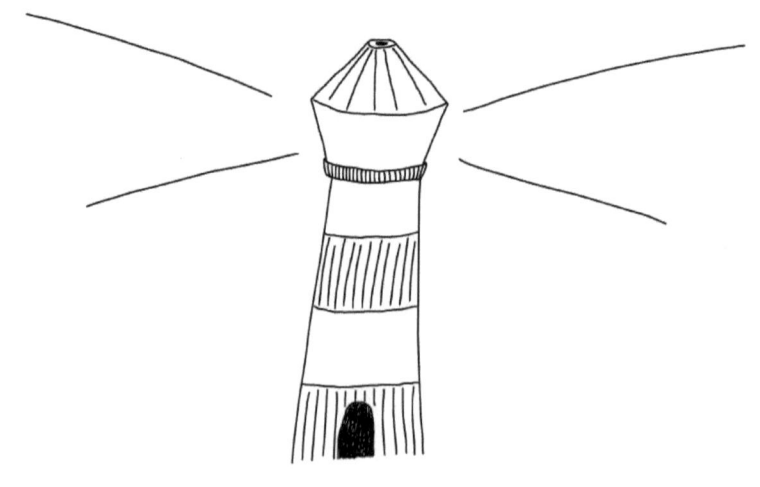

## Lighthouse Love

It was just like a movie, that night
upon the mountain height
Where the wind blew my hair
cheek stroked by freezing winter air

Holding your hand,
with the deep blue sky above,
couldn't help myself from wonder,
is this what they call love?

My heart it starts to pounder,
as I feel your heat
I reach out both my hands
until all our fingers meet

It was just like a movie, that night
with beam from house of light
Where the waves met the shore
and it was you that I fell for

-s

# The game called life

Sometimes you win and sometimes you lose,
it may leave a bruise, it might change your views
But at least you'll heal, you know

it may feel too real, like too big of a deal
Though it's gonna be alright, you know
just hold on tight, to that tiny little light

And soon you'll see, you know
that life is free and full of glee
Just trust me, wait and see

-s

# You said you didn't want me

You said you didn't want me,
and for once it didn't hurt
for I am worth much more,
then to get thrown in the dirt

I am a grown up woman,
not a girl in short short skirt
for I am worth the real love,
and not a summer flirt

You said you didn't want me,
and for once it felt okay
for I can trust myself now,
I'm not compelled to stay

I've come to my right senses,
don't feel the need to play
for you are not my alpha,
and I am not your prey

You said you didn't want me,
and for once I didn't cry
for I have learned my lesson,
you're not my type of guy

I've grown a lot this past year,
now I'm no longer shy
for life is constant changing,
and at least I gave it a try

-s

# Spring

Spring is here, now's the year
sun in sky, today I'll try
Try to thrive, try to strive
be my best, flee the nest

In the sun, have some fun
breath the air, feet are bare
Feel the breeze, climb the trees
like it should, life is good

-s

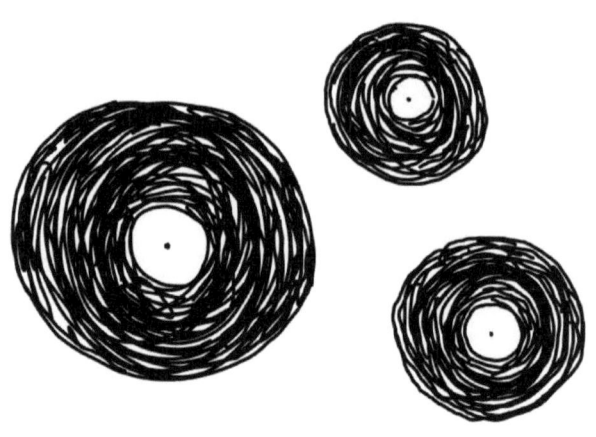

# The sounds of childhood

There's something so familiar,
when you hear a record play
The sounds of your childhood,
longtime back in the day

The crackle of Madonna,
the Beatles and of Queen
The tones of Mamma Mia,
Forever Young and Billie Jean

Though memories from past,
fill our eyes with joyful tears
The whole house filled with happiness,
as the melody reaches our ears

-s

# Do I really like him?

I long for his body, I long for his presence
I long for his smile, I long for his essence

But do I really like him, the way that he loves
me? Am I the perfect girl that he wants me to be?

Should I really, continue on this thing?
Or see what the world instead to me could bring?

Should I lock myself up, to be with this man?
Or should I let go and stick to the plan?

I have my doubts, I have my troubles
I have this feeling without the bubbles

No magic and sparkle, no fairytale dust
Just getting the feeling of things that I must

Though still;
I long for his body, I long for his presence
I long for his smile, I long for his essence

So, what in the world should I actually do?
Find someone else, or just simply get through?

-s

# Woman's issue

Pussy is bleeding,
like the tears from my eyes
the blood has been spread
all over my thighs

Emotions are draining,
I don't know what's real
All the other people saying
it's not that big a deal

Stomach is cramping,
my head it hurts like hell
I get down on my knees
and all I do is yell

But nobody listens,
of course and why would they?
There is nothing to do
 and nothing they could say

For I'm just a woman,
just an ordinary one
and this is just something
that all women gets done

Nothing to share,
or even talk about
It is a woman's issue,
no doubt no doubt

-s

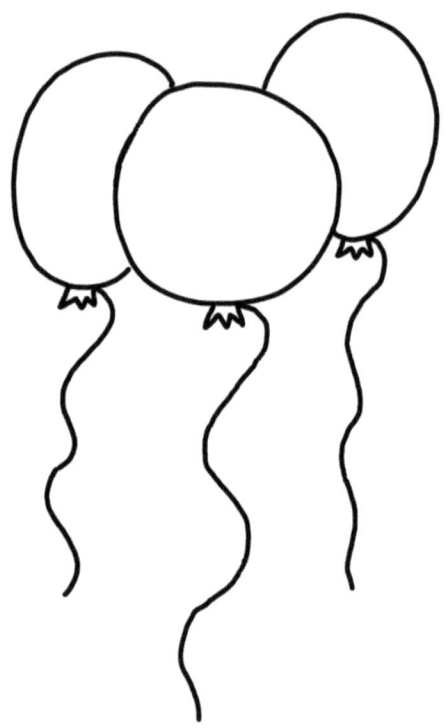

# What happened to the little girl?

What happened to the little girl?
The girl who used to twirl,
the girl with hair of curl?

The girl with glitter in her eyes,
the girl who used to paint the skies

What happened to the little child?
The child who always smiled,
the child who was too wild?

The child whose laughter filled the room,
the child whose flowers always bloomed

Oh dear, life's just got ahead,
the girl is now a memory red
Now everything, it seems so dark,
and everything has lost its spark

Yeah, life sure did leave its scar
and that is why the girl now are
Alone and scarred in this big world
with no hair curled and no skirt twirled

-s

# Again

I've got this urge to take a knife
and cut the bad things out my life

To kill the cloud over my head
see the cuts and watch them bled

To finally could breathe again
through the hurt, through the pain

Then all will be good for a while
I'll walk around at school and smile

Until the day it all goes wrong
I'll try my best to keep my strong

Then find myself there on the floor
with knife in hand to cut some more

-s

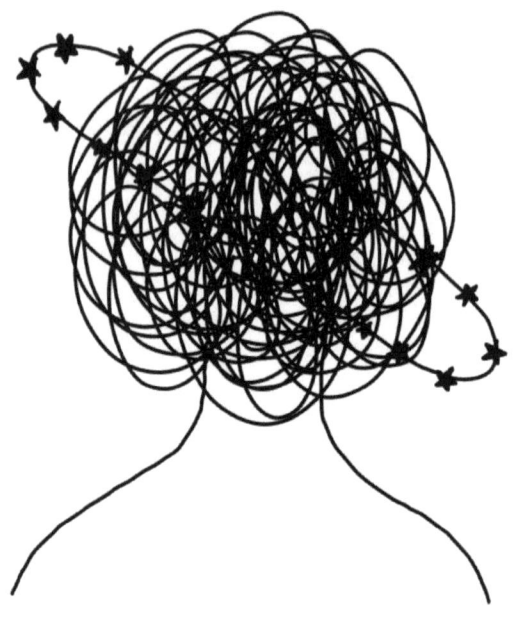

## Better

My body is surrounded,
by this large and angry cloud,
My mind is full of worry
and this fog I can't deny

But somewhere in the distance
I see the light ahead,
I feel the warmth of summer
I smell the flowerbed

Even though the cloud
comes back to me sometimes,
And the fog still eats my brain
I know my future will be bright

I've just got to wait

-s

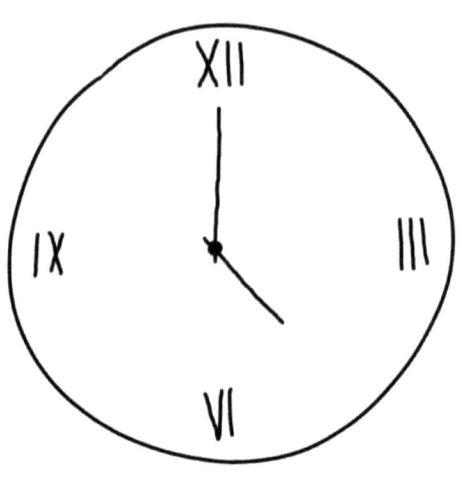

## Pleasure

The pleasure of a woman,
is something quite unique
So how come it is something,
about too taboo to speak?

It begins deep down inside,
then comes tingling up the toes
As the clock's ticking slower,
the faster feeling grows

The waves feel like music,
like tones the waves all come
They're frequent like a rhythm,
of a hard rock band with drum

When the thunderstorm has rendered,
and the lungs gets filled with air
The skin's feeling soft,
you've might just shred a pair

The pleasure of a woman,
is something quite unique
So how come it is the male one,
of who we always speak?

-s

# Body of a goddess

I don't feel satisfied
When I look at my body
I don't stand up with pride
When I look at my body

The great women of Greek
Just then I remember
They weren't all too sleek
Just then I remember

My fatty thighs who's thick
The goddess had them too
My waist who's like a stick
The goddess had it too

When I feel bad about my hips
I look back in bygone times
Watch the women's lips
Back in the bygone times

I'm beautiful and strong
The women mouth at me
I've been that all along
The women mouth at me

-s

## I'm a seven

I'm a seven, yes I'm sure,
don't tell me otherwise

Back in high school; girls got rated
by the cool and popular guys

My C-cup boobs are average
My small waist is divine
My hips are large and sexy
My butt is nice and fine

I'm a seven, yes I know,
though deep down I feel like three

My self esteem so low,
but that's just a part of me

My forehead way to big
My thighs has some stretch marks
My nose is kind of chunky
My eyes don't have the sparks

-s

# The land far away

I want to put on a flowy, summer dress
Run throughout the forest, where the birds all
build their nests

I really want to weave, a vibrant flower wreath
Swim through stormy river, while I escape great
death

I want to feel the sunshine, heat up my pale, bare
skin
Smell the newborn poppies, where the rock has
always been

I want to seek the fairies, of the land so far away
Meet the wild, kind horses, who all they do is
neigh

I want to hear the crickets, in sing and in shout
Water the new seedlings, who'll soon begins to
sprout

I want to stay in this world, for a little while
Fantasies are so much better, than my day to day
lifestyle

-s

## My year

This was gonna be my year
on New Year's Eve it was all I could hear

But things don't always go to plan
even though I do everything I can

Firstly: I failed my driver's test
came like a shock, could never have guessed

Second: I got a D in math
life went on in a different path

Third: I moved away from you
now I only feel so blue

This was gonna be my year
and it will, when I finally get away from here

-s

# Flower bouquet

Life is filled with ups and downs
great surprise and turnarounds

Some days life is sweet and soar
others I just wish for more

Every minute every hour;
each day is like a different flower

Daisy is for the great days,
rose is for the endless maze

Lily for the days of thrill,
tulip for the days of still

Each color; a feeling portray
life is like a flower bouquet

-s

## Acknowledgements

While writing all those poems I was lucky to have so many close friends to share them with; friends who encouraged me to keep writing even when I didn't feel like it.

I want to thank Tore Ek, my No. 1 source of encouragement during this process. But I also want to thank all the people who I wrote those poems about: William Karlsson, Oscar Strickland, Ivar Ottermo, Jonathan Carlsson, Lisa Arneberg, and others.

In some way or another I would also like to thank myself for never giving up on my dream. Without a determined state of mind I would never have been able to publish this collection of poems.

And lastly, I want to thank you, the reader, who picked up *a bouquet of poems*. I hope you found what you were looking for and I hope you enjoyed reading this collection.

-s

# About the author

Sara Arneberg is a
nineteen year old girl born
and raised in the south of
Sweden. She began writing
short stories as early as
elementary school and
continued throughout
middle school. However, it
was not until the later
years of high school that
she found a passion for
writing poetry.

The difficult times at high school were what
began the poetry writing for Sara. Like a
coincidence, she turned to writing as a way to
cope with her emotions. Even though she did not
realize it back then, her poems would soon
become a success amongst her friends and
family.

Now she is debuting with "a bouquet of poems"
which contains a complete collection of poems
written during her junior and senior years of high
school. With titles such as "Lighthouse Love",
"Apple pie" and "Woman's Issue" this work is
like a rollercoaster of emotions. From dark
depressing thoughts to feminist frustration and
deep love stories, this collection has it all.